BLISSFUL RAMBLES

DEVI PRASAD JUVVADI

BLUEROSE PUBLISHERS
India | U.K.

Copyright © Devi Prasad Juvvadi 2023

All rights reserved by author. No part of this publication may be reproduced, stored in a retrieval system or transmitted in any form or by any means, electronic, mechanical, photocopying, recording or otherwise, without the prior permission of the author. Although every precaution has been taken to verify the accuracy of the information contained herein, the publisher assume no responsibility for any errors or omissions. No liability is assumed for damages that may result from the use of information contained within.

BlueRose Publishers takes no responsibility for any damages, losses, or liabilities that may arise from the use or misuse of the information, products, or services provided in this publication.

For permissions requests or inquiries regarding this publication,
please contact:

BLUEROSE PUBLISHERS
www.BlueRoseONE.com
info@bluerosepublishers.com
+91 8882 898 898
+4407342408967

ISBN: 978-93-5741-583-5

Typesetting: Pooja Sharma

First Edition: July 2023

GIFT

To my wife

ANANTHA

Who has been sharing life and

bearing me for over four decades

With love

- Devi Prasad

Acknowledgements

I would like to acknowledge the help of all the persons involved in bringing out "Viswa Vihaaram", my Telugu poetic travelogue into English. Without their encouragement and support, this book would not have become a reality. First, it began with initial encouragement from Mr. Sane Shiva Shankar, Senior Lecturer at NTR Degree College for Women, Mahbubnagar. Then Mr. Srikanth, Associate Professor of English, Govt. City College, Hyderabad was enormously helpful in improving the draft into free verse. I convey my sincere gratitude to both of them.

I would like to thank Dr. Nagaraju Surendra (Elanaaga) for refining this final version, reviewing and writing the foreword to "Blissful Rambles". Many thanks as well to Prof. K. Damodar Rao, former Head, Department of English at Kakatiya University, Warangal for his wise counsel in finalizing the title of the book. However, final responsibility is mine for any errors of fact or interpretation in the book.

- Devi Prasad Juvvadi

Foreword

A Delectable Depiction of World Countries

Travelogues usually take the form of prose, meaning they are written in the form of essays. However, rarely do some poets put their travel experiences in poems, which can then be collectively called poetry travelogues. Long ago, very few people used to visit world countries from India. Hence not many poets who could go on world tour were found. However, the scenario has changed now; more people are embarking upon world tours these days, thanks to the IT boom which enabled many to do so. Yet, the number of poets who write their travel experiences in poetry is still considerably small.

Devi Prasad Juvvadi is one fortunate person who visited many countries in the world. What is more heartening is that he made use of the opportunity to pen his feelings about those countries in the form of poems. First, he wrote them in Telugu language and published in the form of a book titled 'Vishwa Vihaaram'. He is now bringing out a self-rendering of it in English with the title, 'Blissful Rambles'. That way, he may perhaps be regarded as the first poet from Telugu land to write a poetry travelogue. His observations comprise the beautiful panoramic scenes, socio-political situations, and the natures of people of those countries.

There are 64 poems in this book. Except a couple of them, which were composed on his grandchildren, all the others are about different countries of the world. The titles of poems mostly comprise names of the countries, but short caption-like phrases appear just below the titles. They epitomize the essence of those places. This method is somewhat novel and refreshing. For instance, Australia is the main title; *A Tourist's Pleasure* is the short caption below it. Other captions are appealing as well. *Address for Development* (Singapore), *Like Mom* (Sonara Angel), *Inclination for Development* (Shanghai), *Beyond Imagination* (Grand canyon), *Democratic Voice Heard* (South Africa), *Sleepless City* (New York), *The City God Built for Himself* (Varanasi), *Dumb Witness* (Berlin Wall), *Throne of Ideals* (Belgium), and *Address to Royalty* (Palmyra) are some worth mentioning captions.

Writing about Hong Kong, the poet remarks thus:

The bubbling desire for democracy is seen boiling

Hong Kong blinks in the dark horizon of China

Along the coast of fragrance a tragic happiness

The poem *Noisiness of Telugu Associations* is replete with sarcasm. How the association meetings are misused for boozing and flaunting their attire, wealth etc. is depicted well. Read the following lines:

Initially it is TANA

Later ATA, BATA, TATA, NATA, Not...

Similar ones have come up!

He concludes the poem with this facetious observation:

In America,

The Telugu Societies have been infected with pest.

What has been achieved by each society?

How much one earns in them?

The sin of such persons

Needs to be known to the Telugu immigrants!

About Palmyra he says:

Palmyra is a city that died long ago

Today it is a lifeless artifact!

The poet describes Saudi Arabia as a home for peace. To buttress his claim, he gives a long list of undesirable things that are absent in that country. The list comprises political gimmicks, drugs, rapes, black market, adulteration of foods, price hikes, devastating terrorism, agitations, half-naked dances, prostitution, bribery, land scams and so on.

Remarking about Rome: "The dust merges here with aesthetic pleasure, displays the country's bygone." Also, he showers praise on Belgium. See what he says about it:

O Belgium!

You happen to be the care of address

For self-confidence and pure devotion

A home for destitutes,

A throne for ideals.

The poet feels that Switzerland is a place of knowledge.

Despite mountains are lifeless

They stand as wall against greed and hatred of humans

It is a place of prudence

Where love, peace and brotherhood prevail, he says.

See how he concludes hos poem on Berlin Wall:

That erected wall symbolizes their revenge

It is historical one that witnesses man's murkiness silently

A hopeless, lifeless wall built with boulders

Is said to be the wall of Berlin.

A reader, after reading this book completely, garners at least some knowledge about the geographic, natural, and socio-political composition of those countries. That way, the poet has achieved some success in his attempt. I compliment him for the same. At the same time, I am grateful to him for asking me to pen this brief foreword.

Hyderabad — Elanaaga
December 31, 2022 **(Dr. Surendra Nagaraju)**

The Way to the World

(The Poetic Journey of a World Traveller)

After reading the travel poems of Mr. Juvvadi Devi Prasad, 'Blissful Rambles', I am reminded of an Urdu poem (sher) by the renowned Sufi poet Khwaja Mir Dard.

"Sair kar duniyaki gaafil
Zindagani phir kahan
Zindagi agar kuch rahito
Naujawani phir kahan"
(Travel around the world, oh ignorant one!
Where will you find your life again?
Even if there is a bit life left
Will you get your youth back?")

Mr. Juvvadi has fulfilled his life's purpose. He has spent almost half of his life travelling. In my childhood, I was thrilled to read the translation of the French book *Around the World in Eighty days*. Later, it came out as a picture as well, I think. Similarly, I keep re-reading *Kashi yatra* (1831) by Mr. Enugula Veeraswamy. I love reading almost all the Telugu travel books. I have been up-to-date till the recent book *China Yatra* written by

Dr. Gopi, former Vice Chancellor of Telugu University. In fact, I gave lectures on travel history multiple times in Orientation/Refresher Courses. I was instrumental in introducing it as a genre in Telugu syllabus. In this regard, Dr. Machha Haridasu, who was the first one to take up research on travel histories, was my inspiration.

For us Indians, travel experiences are not something new! Our epics like Ramayana and great literary works like Meghasandesam and Manucharitra deal predominantly with travel. In India, crores of people undertake travel. But only some creative minds put their experiences on paper. The more talented lot, focusing on emotion, bring the picturesque places to life in poetry. Our Juvvadi is one such imagination-filled, emotion-laden traveller. He has converted his travels into experiences and feelings in poetic form. He put them in the hands of the readers like someone peeling the banana skin and directly putting the fruit in our hands. He has happily won over their hearts. As for me, this travel poetry has delighted me to no end. I was able to move, unseen, along with the writer and enjoy many scenic experiences.

Since 'Blissful Rambles' is in the free verse format, readers can easily taste the sweetness of a delicious pudding while reading it. Not just that, the book is a treasure trove for those who haven't been on a world tour. Further, it is like a beacon of light for enthusiasts undertaking world travels.

There are many poems that I loved in this travel collection. KARACHI- City under military shadows, SAUDI ARABIA-The Home of Peace, AFRICA-The Diversity of Life, LAS VEGAS- The Place where Golden Coins Harvest, JOHANNASBURG-The Golden City with the Black Sun and I could go on with the list of poems that haunt. Mainly, in our indigenous travel poems: KOLKATA- The Synergy of Equality and Love, VARANASI- The city God built for himself impressed me most. Gyanapeeth awardee Kedar Nath Singh had written a great poem called 'Banaras'. Devaraju Maharaju Garu had translated the poem with similar, great gusto.

This poetic compilation of travel memoir by Juvvadi if and when translated into any Indian language will leave the readers mesmerized. Moreover, we are in great need of translation literature as well.

Reading the poems about his granddaughters in this book made my heart rejoice! The poems on REVA and ROOHI are unforgettable. 'Ruh' means 'soul'; the name 'Roohi' comes from that word. Coming to the poem SONARA ANGEL, the poet managed to convey his love for his mother. The poem on his grandson, 'DIVINITY IN GODLINESS', managed to disclose divine secrets in a spiritual way. While writing the 'Blissful Vignettes' world travel memoirs, the poet Juvvadi must have seen numerous beauties that must have captivated him. But the fact that he has managed to steer clear of the romantic angle and maintain balance speaks volumes about his wisdom, or maybe the credit goes to the fact that his wife was with him. Because we meet any number of people when we travel especially on foreign trips. Some people tend to come quite close to us. I found this phenomenon in foreign lands. An anonymous Urdu poet had written a poem (sher) on this aspect. It has since been used multiple times in movies.

"Raah mein unse
Mulakat ho gayi
Jise hum darte the
Vahi baat ho gai"
(I met her
on my way
What I was afraid might happen
Has happened, somehow)

This world traveller should be hale and hearty for a long, long time. We should have the opportunity to read many more such writings by him. I hope his works would touch the peaks of travel literature bringing laurels to him in the form of accolades and many awards.

Dear travel aficionados, travel around the world without spending a dime, without straining your legs, by getting on the plane of words with 'Blissful Rambles'. See the beauties of foreign lands without the hurdles of visas! Feel the world! Give your compliments to Juvvadi who has presented us with such a great travel book. Let us congratulate him!

Prof. Endluri Sudhakar
Telugu Department
Hyderabad University

12 December 2019

Captivating Poetic Experience

While saying "Poetry is unquenchable thirst" and "Nothing is a taboo for poetic material" the famous Telugu poet Sri Sri had given a direction to the world of poetry long time ago. "Who are the workers that lifted stones for the Taj"? he asked and advised the readers to recognise the labour hidden behind the wonders of the world. That way he made these monuments an integral part of poetry.

Undertaking travels is not new for us. But traditionally we are used to pilgrimages. The pioneer of travel waiting in Telugu, Enugula Veeraswamy too depicted different places he had visited on his way to many temple towns. In the process, he gave a good account of his travel history. In this genre, Prof. Nayani Krishnakumari's *Kashmira Deepakalika* is a noteworthy book. Not so well-educated film actor, Akkineni Nageshwar Rao wrote his America travel experiences thus earning a prominent place in Telugu trave writings. All the eminent litterateurs have made it a point to record the places, towns, and monuments they had visited in their unique style.

This book is different from the travel literature appeared so far in Telugu. The surname 'Juvvadi' reminded me of Karimnagar-based Juvvadi Gautham Rao, the protégé of eminent poet Vishwanatha Satyanarayana and the one who rendered his mentor's *Srimad Ramayana Kalpavriksham* melodiously. He also happened to be editor, critic in his own right. Along with the surname, Juvvadi Devi Prasad possesses similar talent and has attracted international fame. With studies in three countries, professional service in six countries Sri Devi Prasad proved himself to be truly a world traveller while undertaking travels to over thirty six countries as avocation as also part of his vocation. It is commendable that that he has selected poetic medium for expressing his experiences! He portrayed the important details of different countries, some world-famous leaders and also his blood relations endearingly. Similarly, he had exposed the rot of America Telugu associations.

He described Jerusalem as

Thou were the city of knights in yore

Thou were the city of beautiful livelihood

A flagship of poetry in history

In modern era, a promising compass of the future

Burj Dubai as

In the mid-afternoon there where the tall tower touching the sky like a magical wand is seen glistening in the brightness of sunlight

It twinkles all along the day

During the dusk twinkling of lights, gears up for feats

In the nights, the rise of waterfalls mingles with lights

Amidst the soft sand

This is possible if only one has a firm command over world history, on matters of political, economic and cultural importance. It becomes apparent from his poems that Sri Devi Prasad could accomplish this by keeping himself abreast of persons, places and poetry of the respective countries.

It is a rare thing to bring out a collection of poems written over so many countries. I think this is first such attempt. Sri Devi Prasad lived in a number of countries for many years, also presented papers on science and technology, authored books on those subjects, but his love for Telugu is evident in these poems! These beautiful poems bear testimony to his literary commitment.

The title of the poem, *Blissful Rambles* is quite appropriate. This is a journey of the poet as a world traveller who has shared with us his feelings and experiences laced with captivating descriptions. One hopes that this poetic account of world travel would, in all likelihood, provide inspiration in myriad ways to many writers and contribute to the thrust in world tourism.

I earnestly hope that Sri Devi Prasad would bring out many more books in future. Welcome to the poetic world of Sri Devi Prasad.

15 December 2019 **Cheekolu Sundaraiah**
Hyderabad **Poet and Author**

About My Global Travels!

On the release of my first poetry collection, I want to share some words about myself and the background of these poems.

My childhood was spent in a small village on the banks of Godavari river, near the temple town of Dharmapuri in the united Karimnagar district of Telangana state. My father, Yashwant Rao, used to recite poems melodiously during the nights. My mother, Narasamma, not only read the epics Ramayana, Bharatham, Bhagavatam, but also used to read the Andhra Prabha weekly newspaper, which she used to subscribe back in 1960s. Maybe, that background inculcated my interest in poetry!

After completing my schooling in Telugu medium, I had to shift to Hyderabad for further studies. Because of that, I made attempts to master English language. However, I continued to attend gatherings of Telugu poets and literary meetings whenever I could find time. During that time, I met several poets and writers. This facilitated me to read a wide variety of books. Although I used to send a few of my poems to magazines, I didn't write much. Before I could work towards fulfilling my ardent wish to write poetry at some point of time, I had to go abroad for higher studies.

After going overseas, everything, from my jobs, my marriage with Anantha Laxmi, two beautiful children, Sreekar and Mahathi, happened quite naturally. My occupation made me spend most of my time in the Middle East countries. Due to a sound financial position, I used to take my family to different countries during vacations every year. In fact, my father used to joke that we could have bought 100 acres of land in the vicinity of Hyderabad with the amount of money that we had spent on our trips about three or four decades back. But what did the world-conqueror Alexander take with him when he died? We must live our lives the way we want to! If possible, we must make history or make a name for ourselves in the history books.

The world is quite vast. It is a motley collection of so many strange and different things. Each country has something unique about it. I had opportunities very early to see many countries and their natural wonders, historical places, buildings, cultural epitomes, forests, mountains, waterfalls, rivers, cities, modern buildings, etc. Even professionally as well, I had the opportunity to visit many countries. I had the good fortune to meet many celebrities in few countries. Whichever tour I undertook, I had the habit of writing whatever I felt about the places I saw and the people I met. In those days, photography was a costly affair. So, I used to use Ekta chrome slides. After the trips, we used to invite our colleagues for dinners on weekends and show them the slides on a projector and share the highlights of my trips.

In truth, the one who inspired my idea of writing poetry, not exactly on love, revolutions and ideology, but rather on themes like cities, countries, etc. was the world-renowned poet Faiz Ahmed Faiz. Back in the late 70s, I chanced upon meeting the great poet himself while I was working in the American University of Beirut as an Assistant Professor. In a way, his poem on the Beirut city called 'Beirut - Ornament of the World' could be described as inspiration to this compilation.

I hadn't written any of these poems with particular focus on poetic language, style etc. Without having a firm grip on the language, I tried to express my feelings through these poems. To a sensitive and responsive soul, every poem is a melody—by looking at it from the poet's perspective. No two people's experiences are the same! But one thing is true—the 'Blissful Rambles' world travel memoirs compilation is my modest attempt at recording my random writings during my travels and share my joys with you before the words fade away and the papers get torn. The following poem tries to make my experience a collective experience:

The blooming of nature's beauty

The fragrance of the sweet-smelling coral jasmine

The enchanting melodious songs of Squil

The riveting river of moonlight.

The present collection is:

The musical flow of my global excursion

The rendering of many years has transformed into words today

I wrote down what I felt apt

I aspire to steal your heart with it.

I hope that the first attempt in my English literary tour called 'Blissful Rambles' would leave you entertained to the core. This is not the history of the countries and cities of this world! It is about my wanderings, my experiences, my fond memories of this vast world.

This book is my endeavour to stand on my own on the stage of poetry. I hope that after reading my book you will give me constructive criticism and advice to further improve my writing since the jury for any book are its readers.

18 December 2019   **Devi Prasad Juvvadi**

Hyderabad

Travels

1. Malaysia 1
2. China 3
3. The Great Wall Of China 7
4. Hongkong 9
5. Macao 13
6. Minnesota Star 15
7. Noisiness of Telugu Associations 17
8. Divineness 23
9. Istanbul 25
10. Jerusalem 27
11. Bethlehem 29
12. Australia 33
13. Singapore 35
14. Sonora Angel 37
15. Shanghai 38
16. Grand Canyon 39
17. Las Vegas 43
18. Minnesota 45
19. Minneapolis 47
20. Roohi 49
21. Burj Dubai 51
22. Brazil 53
23. Johannesburg 55

24. Cape Town 57
25. South Africa 61
26. Simla 63
27. St. Louis 65
28. Niagara 67
29. New York 69
30. Varanasi 72
31. Kolkata 75
32. Karachi 77
33. Vienna 81
34. Danube River 83
35. Munich 85
36. Cologne 87
37. The Berlin Wall 89
38. Geneva 91
39. Switzerland 93
40. Copenhagen 95
41. Amsterdam 97
42. Belgium 99
43. Paris 101
44. Versailles Palace 104
45. London 106
46. Thames 108
47. Rome 110
48. Florence 112

49. Kashmir 114
50. Bangkok 117
51. Philippines 119
52. Mecca 121
53. Sandstorms 123
54. Saudi Arabia 125
55. Africa 128
56. Sudan 130
57. Yasser Arafat 132
58. George Habash 134
59. Petra 136
60. Cyprus 138
61. Palmyra 141
62. Faiz Ahmed Faiz 143
63. Beirut 145
64. Lebanon 147

1. Malaysia

Elegant Country

Embellished with beauteous mountains, rivers, valleys, thick forests

Historical greatness and radiant sunrays

A flourishing nation this is.

Here, all people are one country, one soul and one body

They help make the nation march on the path of progress.

In this nation, there are Indians, Chinese,

British, Australians and Americans.

Russians too happen to inhabit here.

Irrespective of religion, colour, and nationality

Many had shed blood for this nation

Despite hailing from different roots and religions

They are eager to achieve unity in diversity

The Twin Towers, "Petronas"

Were once the tallest buildings of the world.

Edifices of Kaula Lumpur brought splendour to it

Kuala Lumpur
27 November 2018

2. China

Racing in progress

China!

You and India are the oldest civilized countries

Both hold great inheritance of cultures

Ten centuries ago we both were equal participants

In achieving supremacy in the world

And hundred years ago

We two have faced the slavery under colonialism

And both fought against foreign rule

So as to enter into the world of freedom

Despite our chosen paths of us are different

The dream of freedom is being achieved at the same period.

Even in our march towards development our chosen paths are different

But the famine and its darkling dance

The cry and the fury of poverty

Are the comrades to both of us in our cherished journeys

Having been sharpening both to pen and sword

'Mao" paves way for another world for you

While "Mahatma" treading on the path of democracy in democratic manner

Puts on the steps towards 'village governance'

But with no change in the generation thy reputation has changed

Thy development has spread across the world like a dragon

The fragrance of thy very progress is seen striking our nostrils

Like anybody else we couldn't believe it

It is said that the progress is of dictators and repression

And of such one's, does not sustain for long is the prediction

Despite our goal of is same but the path of march is different

When you stand in the path of progress

I couldn't remain calm but appreciate you

Be it in the development of food items, be it in industries

for the matter of creating of wealth, in all of them, you are in forefront

it matters not whether a cat is black or white

what matters is that whether it catches rats or not

with the principle of " Deng Xiaoping "

four decades ago on the frontiers of Shanghai

in "Mehan Shan" amidst bamboo forest

being inaugurated by the economists

thy progress path, planning, execution

have been kissing the sky and surprising everyone

having been enhancing the capacity and distributing equality

you are on the run

but our communists

are still clinging to the outdated salutation of "Red Salutes"

not inviting the cherished change either

Beijing

10 ovember 2016

3. The Great Wall Of China

Built by the monarchies of generations

As a fort of resistance against invasion of foes

Thy aim to obliterate them for over two thousand years

Holding in two hands as well as shouldering boulders on thy neck

The Chinese criminals, Soliders have built this gorgeous wall

By the Golden arrows

The Chinese Empire has been divided into two

Both Mangolian soldiers as well as horses were wounded and went away

But 8851 kilometer spread the Great wall of China

Still persists tall without much damage

Has been mocking the world

Like the tail of dragon is seen spreading over

Has been crawling on the mountains

Even makes one forget the scorching sun.

Beijing
12 November 2016

4. Hongkong

The city of dreams

One country bearing two policies
The threshold of China
And holds special zone of governance
A garland of several sects and creeds
Desires queue up in the sky over here
It is a city that unveils the ways of opportunities
The centre for international entrepreneurship
The roads glitter under Neon lamps
It holds costly congregation of buildings
Royal cottages for entertainment
Attractive and elegant looking girls
Enthuse one's youthful feelings
A memoir of sweet emotions

The bubbling desire for democracy is seen boiling
Hongkong blinks in the dark horizon of China
Along the coast of fragrance a tragic happiness
Oh! City of dreams

Where would be your travel to? What would be your destination?

Hongkong

13 November 2016

5. Macao

Unsealed casinos

The city which has been forgotten by all, over generations
Today, as "Las Vegas of China" it is popular
Whole city glitters with brightness
Streets are seen embellished with "Colourful Lights"
Amidst sand and pebbles
And in the path of pedestrians
Our very shadows become amphibians
There, where never be clubs be closed
Opium drinks, catwalk of girls
Erotic exposure in nude dances
In the gambling, every one imagines to be intelligent
Yet, believes in fortune
Each one of the intelligent
Such one begins the game with a single coin
Greed enhances the range of gambling
He plays on, till he breaks down on to his knees
At last he empties his purse
If this addiction crosses the limits
He will end up as a bankrupt

Macao
14 November 2016

6. Minnesota Star

Destination of love

The blossomed lily in the azure sky
Thou rare bhidhiya on earth
Kaleidoscopes beauty of infinite stars
The blinking star of yapolis during dew showered night
Thou are credited like star Revathi which beautifies the sky

O Reva, my grandchild!
Thy very arrival brings forth spring of tender mango leaves
Have added the relish of happiness in our family
Thy beam of light comes from dews capes
Has pictured onto us the glitter of thousands stars
And the jasmines have been heard melodiously
The path is perched by octave chords
Has gifted us the affectionate welcome

(My feelings when I first saw our granddaughter)

Fairfax, Virginia
3 July 2016

7. Noisiness of Telugu Associations

In America many Telugu Societies

On which no limitations, no control is seen executed

All of which mean nothing

Initially it is TANA

So forth every one indulged in flattery

Later on

ATA, BATA, TATA, NATA, NOT ...... similar ones have come

Whatever might be the name for the matter

Without any name of the caste

All such societies are prone to caste and family politics

Each of it possesses a godfather

And consists of some patrons

And some other holds permanent membership

Each one of it strives to keep its identity

When one sees further

In all these Telugu societies

Say Congress , Telugu Desham, TRS, YSRC

Telangana, Andhra differences do exist among them

As far as the matter of Chandra Babu and Jagan is concerned
Irrespective of regional issues
Irrespective of issues of political parties
The unity of castes is flourishing
During the nights, liquor parties take place
On the occasions of Telugu festivals
Every body shares the warmth of unity
But in the elections
Who will stand on whose side?
Only the Lord of Petersburg knows it
In the societies hardly any work exists
But there lies a competition for the designations
Every a year there are dinners in five star motels
For raising funds
Rooster crowed conferences were being convened
For goodness sake every year
They hold Independence and Republic Days
Meetings, assemblies, patriotic songs as such
Now and then
For people like Anna Hazare
For movements against graft
They announce their support

There will be parades in the park
In celebrations of Telugu festivals
Literary meetings, the ladies
In the saris of Chandana, Bommana brands
Being decorated in diamond jewelery
With ten carets of gold
The ladies display elegance
And convene beauty pagans
In the dinners, parle on Indian aspects
Where which one says rupees three crores
Were being spent in his brother's daughter marriage
And some other says rupees six crores
Were spent in the reception of his brother's son
On another table
For our sister's daughter
Her sister has spent Rupees ten crores, says one
Some other says, for her sister's son
They have received rupees hundred crores
While the males before they finish their drinks
Many a man become sinking ships
For the sake of Telugu culture
And for conservation of Telugu Arts
In the temples and in the hotels

Dance programmes by children are arranged

Who were being coached by the masters

Of those who were recently been in visit;

cinema stars who have been on shooting schedule

or politicians who have been on private works

sponsored by government

are often chosen as chief guests

and soon after it, they broadcast it in the U-Tubes

Hardly a handful of spectators are present

in the concerts that are convened

in the honour of literary personalities

who happen to pay a visit to see their children

Every a year

they tour in India on the sponsorship of societies

and pretend to work to the bone of boss

hold meetings with a Chief Minister or the Prime Minister, if possible

and deliver speeches in English about the development of Telugu language

In the name of aid for welfare programmes

they lay ladders to the sky

interviews in the TVs

news items in the newspapers

acquaintance programmes with popular people

recommendations for political debuts

annual conferences with crores of expenditure

to get end the two year coloured tenure

there will be songs and dances

exhibiting to the waist of actress Naynatara

and so with the complexion of Thammanna

felicitations to those Indians known to them

accusations of debit and credits

mudslinging against each other and the heated arguments

make one forget the assembly proceedings

In America

The Telugu Societies have been infected with pest

What has been achieved by each society?

How much one earns?

The sin of such persons

Needs to be known to the Telugu immigrants.

>*(Feelings after attending TANA meetings at Santa Clara during 1-3 July 2011,*
>
>*ATA meetings at Chicago during 1-3 July 2016 and*
>
>*American Telangana Association meetings at Detroit during 8-10 July 2016)*

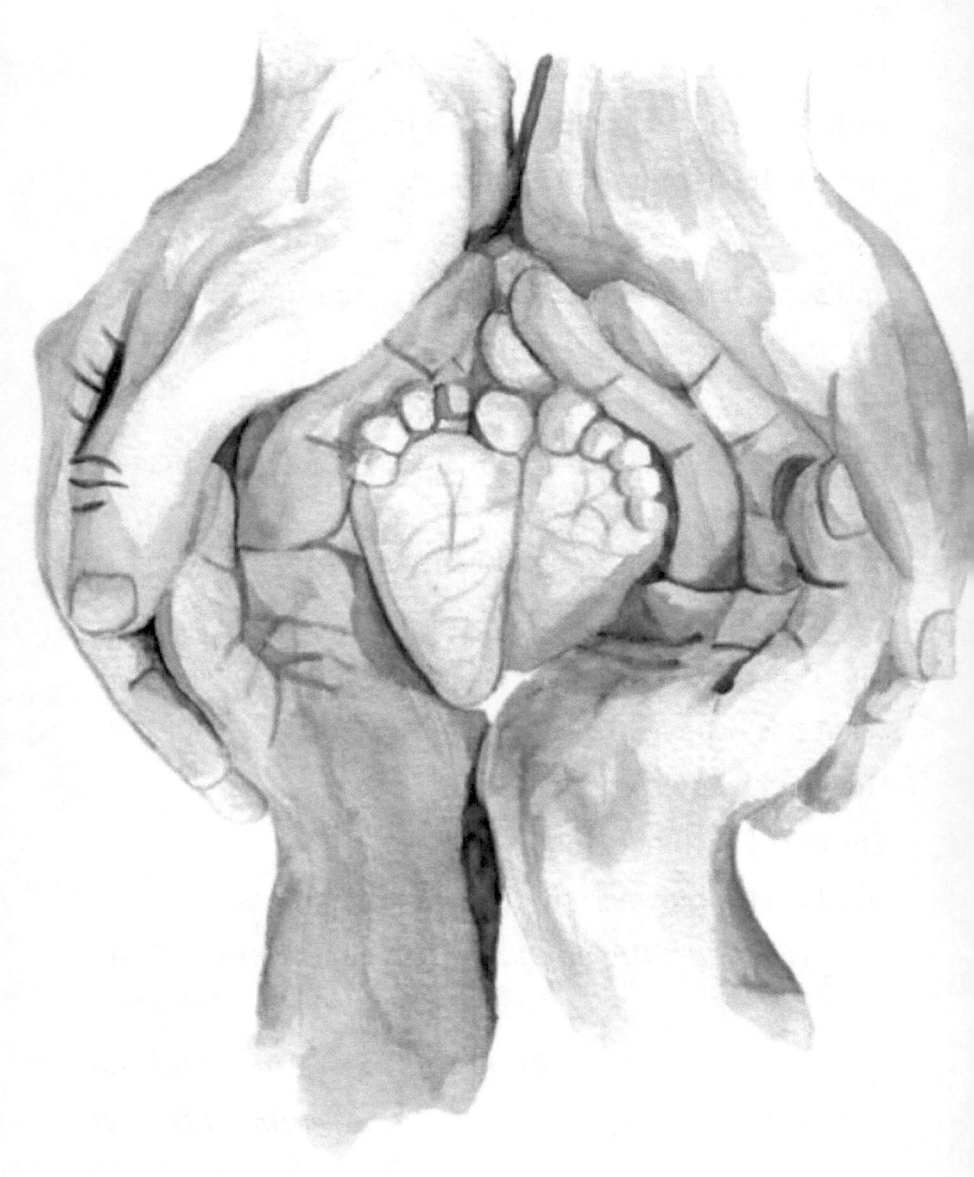

8. Divineness

Godliness in grandson

Such one

Is said to be God

He who descends from azure sky

On to the earthly lap

With his very step in this infinite sky

Does shower smile

With magical and jubilant feats

He makes one feel happy and also mesmerized

Such one fellow is God

Has opened his eyes

The whole world is seen embracing moonlight

He is God

Has opened his mouth

Upon which the little Krishna's little words were heard thus

"Mother, for eating mud I am considered naughty or mad"

Of the very sight of him

Our hearts are filled with memorable feelings

Our lips sang melodious songs

Our souls showered the first rain of the season

Have sparkled up rainbow glitters

Peacocks are seen dancing

Oh ! God I am blessed

His very birth

Does beckon light amidst the darkness

Needs to create the history

Needs to stand tall in the history

Let him be blessed to live for thousands of years

Within the divinity is Godly one

Such one is said to be God

Whoever takes birth in His constellation,

He will be the one who extends our clan

(My feelings when I first saw my grandson)

Phoenix

15 November 2017

9. Istanbul

Perched on seven hills

Thou witness present, past and future generations

Is a city embodied with diversified history

It is said to be a union of Eastern and Western cultures

A piece of mutual agreement between North and South poles

Though takes credit to have spread amidst the two continents

Thou be the threshold of both Asia and Europe

In yesteryears it was Constantinople, Byzantium

But today it is "Istanbul"

Is an aristocratic capital city where hundreds

Of Roman, Byzantium, Latin and Ottoman emperors reigned over

For thousands of Years

This very city is not a city at all but is a fable of the world

Its delicate history makes one's heart bloom

Since past The Sun, The Moon, The Earth and The ocean

All such will be seen to dream over here itself

The city which establishes on Seven hills

Is a home of several specialties

Each hill is a special attraction

"Hagia Sophia" "Sultane Majid",

"Topkapi Palace" "Grand Bazar" "Golden Heart"

Are the excavations of the bygone glory

The place which placidly made live the deaths

of several knights who were victorious

amidst the graves of glittering marble stone

of several beauteous cities in the world

undoubtedly, Istanbul makes one mad with wonder

                                                  Istanbul

                                          25 April 2015

10. Jerusalem

Origin of religions

Jerusalem! Thou were the city of knights in yore

Thou were the city of beautiful livelihood

A flagship of poetry in history

In modern era, a promising compass of the future

It's filled with fragrance of religious angles

A geodesic of worldly paradise

Once, it shone with distinctive culture

Here was cradled the civilization

A city that hosted several religions

It is a city where religion is an addiction

A city with no end at all

That impulsively runs all the time

Is a city where conflicts be never ending

On the day, whole of Jerusalem streets are filled with military men

Children who became destitute, their parents by the side of street

Children with dead parents

Alas ! All of them are the family of Abraham

Where were those people?

Where were those affections?

Jerusalem

27 April 2015

11. Bethlehem

On the dull path

A native place of superstitions

Where religion became a death warrant,

It is a place of three fate-oriented religions

The fence here pierces the very earth

On the either side, in retaliation, were attacks

For over thousands of years

There, death shadows' gloom at each and every step

The crushed flower buds

The auxiliary leaves were wet with blood

The birds devoid of wings

Chaos in the desert

Despite the tourists desire to have a glimpse

Of Bethlehem from a distance

Amidst the thorny path

Our convoy at once got stopped

At check point 300

On 30 feet high walls, the patrolling of

Soldiers, cameras, barbwire barricades

The messages of contemporary political affairs on graphite

Unknowingly an idea flashes in the heart of the very sight of those

Appears blood like a flag

Massacre in the name of bravery

On the other side of the wall the entrance gate of the city

The whole city remained silent at the very entrance

Of Christian star Bethlehem

Christ's birthplace is seen dull and drab

Weird lands

Deserted fruit trees and flowering gardens
Except tickling clock, nothing is moving
It is like a lifeless prison
A dreadful atmosphere
Time never would remain like so, for ever
Is it a crime to visit and have blessings?
Is it a suicide of one's soul?
On this very holy land
A new world should take birth
New springs need to bloom up

Bethlehem
29 April 2015

12. Australia

A Tourist's Pleasure

A vast country

Upon which the rays of morning sun shine brightly

Such a country is Australia

It is a place for several destitute people

A darling country than that of their own people

For those who hail from distant places

"Kangaro" is quite dear to them

All of whom are lovers of bio-diversity

"Gold coast" glitters light up the sky

The hues of water of "Great Barrier Reef"

All of which will enthral the visitors

Old, rain-fed forests

Like jewellery that aids beauty, ocean beaches are seen

Walk on foot amidst the white sand

The feats of migrated whales in a row

All of which fill us with happiness

To rejuvenate the decaying forests

by splitting the grasslands and chasing the rivers

were built the shadowed paths

on the other side of wide plains, are the tore mountains

the white ring bark of axed great forest suffices tragedy

is seen competing with moon

smoke-fed mountains glitter like a blue ruby

this land, this wind, these oceans blush

and around grasslands, fields of crops

the special blooming bush "Harotaf" like a natural fence, it appears

variety of beauteous feats of thou

is a token of earthly love.

Brisbane

26 February 2013

13. Singapore

Address for development

A nation known for

Modern age civilization

Over its sky, features calmness

Embellishes with gorgeous grasslands

A splendid nation endows with cities

A civilized city that forms

Out of faith, sacrifice and bravery for generations

Truthfulness is in thy

Thou are the shining star in streets of the international market

You own economic self-sufficiency

Never are there economic crimes

In the index of growth thy surpass others

Despite dearth of natural resources'

All others will bank on thy

How have you achieved this mark, skill and eligibility in the aspects

Of democracy, Law and order, growth, hygiene,

And standard of living

The growth rate that you achieved

Inspires the people of the world

what did you do to reach it?

And how did you do it?

There lies a secret in this growth of thy

One doesn't know whether this could be attributed to others also

But this growth makes all wonder

Only this feature welcomes one to visit thy.

Singapore
1 March 2013

14. Sonora Angel

Like mom

She is an angel
Thou a blossom of the desert Sonara
Thou are the form of our darling dreams descends
On to the earth from the sky
Thou the angel been floating away from the sky
Been flowing as waterfall in Grand Canyon
You are an epic born from the Kalidasa's pen
Thou are a melody that emerged from Annamayya's tongue
She is my mother Narasamma
Only she is Sreenikha
An angel of Sonara
A portrait of our smiles
Her very onset during sunshine
Has spread out the fragrance around
Has appeased our very eyes
Has filled our souls with happiness

(Feelings when my granddaughter first visited)
Hyderabad, India
20 December 2013

15. Shanghai

Inclination for development

O the great city of Shanghai!

Why are you always dreaming the time of yore?

Have you been expecting the passed out days to come again?

Is a place of cool and calm away from the tumult?

Thou have been longing for a place of aloofness across the ocean

the Chinese's dream of progress is visible now

keeping aside ideals thou have stood for new ideals and new changes

You earned respect in the world

It would like to tread in the path of growth shown by you

Shanghai
24 June 2011

16. Grand Canyon

Beyond imagination

A billion years ago

By the flow along the thick forest

And along the banks of river Colorado

There formed a gorgeous valley

The one sculpted by the very nature

When one watches standing on the cliff

Beneath it is seen a God created

Tens of thousands constructed hue of wealth

There appear cracked caves built with golden walls

They are seen shining exquisitely

The sculpted wealth of stone art carved out of granite

Is seen outdoing than that of the palaces of the kingdoms

And been sustaining for a billion of years

Though flowing fiercely from time immemorial

The river flow is seen faintly

When viewed up amidst the greetings of mountains

A marvellous scene carved out by the brush of omnipresence.

Like the eye of heaven wondrous temple of Lord Vishnu

In the passage of time

There may be a change in geographical outlines

And boundaries in the world

But the beauty of Grand Canyon is beyond imagination

There, calmness, peace with no disturbance

Will fill all of us with exuberance.

Grand Canyon
27 June 2011

17. Las Vegas

Harvest gold coins

A famous city of the world known for pomp and gaiety

An oasis amidst the desert of Nevada

One finds not a drop of water to drink

But gold coins grow in it abundantly

It is a care of address for carnivals, a nest for entertainment

To scoop the merriment

To test one's fortune

The visitors flow incessantly into it

Celestial airplanes carry them to their destination

On the arrival of married couples, gala lovers, prostitutes

in the innovative buildings styles of London, Paris, Venice

Gambling continues day and night

Crazy emotions, luxurious lives,

Memorable exotic nights, cheer girls' display of wobbliness

Amidst soporific songs and the exotic dances of ladies

They begin the show with the goal of how much one should earn

Instead of how to earn

Some would be millionaires while some others are beggars in the span of seconds,

In the matter minutes millionaires be becoming bankrupts

Many such millionaires set out for begging

The rainbow dances of nymphs like Rambha, Uravasi, Menaka

Beautiful girls in short, semi-little clothing

Singers, Dancers, spellbinding shows

All streets filled with conflictions

Parade of half- naked girls

In every street

Fools are seen to lose their wisdom in pursuit of lust

In the numbness of wine, the prostitutes forgot the humanity

A world of illusion, a city of dreams

Initially it welcomes one with smiles

But at the end

The crushed beauties

Several scenes of wounded lives

Topsy-turvy journeys of lives

If one loses prudence in Las Vegas

One will skid in one's life; this is a naked truth over here

Las Vegas
30 June 2011

18. Minnesota

Sweet memories

Ye! Minnesota

Has been listening about thee since times

Thou are the darling of our children

Look forward to visit

Thy fresh Air, Lakes, Rivers

Thy golden crops such as wheat and corn

Glitter with the touch of light during dawn

In the azure sky the Northern lights are seen still glowing

Has heard thou have been doing great farming

With amiable cooperation of farmers in thy land

Are they still continuing the same trend?

Isn't the fog upon thy skies calm and untouched by pollution?

Aren't you in the green memory of folklore?

Aren't Norway pines widely grown in thy garden?

Aren't South westerly's passing upon thy trees

In such winds, doesn't the fragrance of flowers still persist?

In the turbulent flow of Minnesota, aren't the boats been seen floating, slowly?

Aren't precious crops, steep mountains, mines, flour mills still in existence?

Right now the falling snow is still seen white and soft

Many people are still be seen migrating

All of them say Minnesota is their native place to this day

For that matter,

Our children who migrated

Love the work place instead of natives

What specialty thou be holding on

Despite the winds blowing at a speed of seventy miles

In spite of minus three degrees centigrade temperature

For over a century people have been living over here

To watch thy secret I am here.

Minneapolis
12 July 2011

19. Minneapolis

City of lakes

Minneapolis is a paradise of union of three rivers

Where sadafur ,pine trees celebrate spring

To exhibit its greatness

The maple trees grow tall to touch the sky

During the nights of winter

When snow showers over the pine trees

It appears as if bunches of stars are dropping from sky

When watching them the following morning

White fog makes the fruit droop

With the onset of the fall season

like a glorious rainbow a variety of trees, plants appears

some wear light green and some dark green

while some other are seen shedding the leaves

and some more are seen with ripped leaves

the very sight of it is a colourful canvas, appeases

has been there a soul to parle, a heart to listen on

it is said that these trees talk too

with the pine trees strewn in groups

the dewdrops of gentle wind will hold talk

and at the city of Lexas takes respite

in souls of trees of unuttered dumb and static one

the grand history of Minniapolis, the roots of thousand conferences

the seeds which infuse life in the colourful trees

the torchbearers of Minnesota

people's aims and aspirations

might have been hidden

the folded mountains

cascading valleys

gentle breezes

shower of craziness

like so, Minneapolis is a concert of enlightenment

a special chord of music

Minneapolis
8 July 2011

20. Roohi

Darling doll

Roohi! O Roohi!
Thou are the soul of many people
And also a sweet dream of many more
Away from continents
And very far away from oceans nine
Thou are the descended star on the land
Thou are the -
Happen to get unveiled in this land of frost
Thou are our very elegance
Thou are our dream girl
Thou are our mother

Having crossed distances, banks
Having come to a cradle function
The very first sight of you
ebbs in me unknown mellifluous emotions, a feeling of love
The very shower of thy smile
Has made me catch up a crore of frosty lights
Thou are glamorous
Thy glamour outshines
the purple moonlight
thou make red roses bloom in one's heart
and make one forget one's grief
elicit one's emotions
ebbs of poesy in ones
thy peel of laughter
decked with gold hue of hibiscus
has been adorned with such melodious flowers
an immense treasure in the times to come
for us thou beckon thousand lamps of lights
thy very smile
is the music, chord, and melody to my poetry
and hereafter throughout the duration of my life
thou are my darling doll, it is none other than you

(Feelings after seeing our first grandchild Roohi)
Minneapolis
11 July 2011

21. Burj Dubai

The pride of Arabs

In the mid-afternoon there where the tall tower touching the sky

like a magical wand is seen glistening in the brightness of sunlight

It twinkles all along the day

During the dusk twinkling of lights, gears up for feats

In the nights, the rise of waterfalls mingles with lights

Amidst the soft sand

The shower of water strives to reach out to stars

A congregation of thick clouds in the sky

Plays hide-and-seek with fog

Makes one feel joyous and mesmerizes
Why this pompous show of royalty?
Thou are seen nodding head as if it is quite possible for you too
So thou are announcing to the world the grandeur of Dubai
Thou are seen piercing towards cosmos
Oh thou are condensed artificiality
Isn't it a sign of our souls flying in the sky?
Oh, thy waterfall dances in air
What an elegance it displays with pure hues!
None can match you in waterfall display
Oh! What a display of gorgeousness!
So splendid is thy popularity
None could achieve thy greatness
Marvellous is thy elegant dance
Thousands of people were blessed, for they visited you
In the tent of star-studded ones
The gush of colourful waterfall display
Oh! The grandeur of Arab
Resembles the heaven on the land
Kudos to thou

Dubai

15 February 2011

22. Brazil

A figurine bestowed by nature

Earth attired in a sari

Is seen embellished with forests, mountains, valleys, waterbodies

She Looks like a decorated golden doll

With wide biodiversity

With excellent waterfalls, with rare wealth of fishes

From yore to the modern period

With pages of history, secret stories, natural disasters

Endows the deep features of mother nature

Amazon forest as an ideal of mankind

As a pragmatic flag it flutters ever
With thousands of clouds
Bundled with corers of droplets
Amazon River flows
To quench the thirst of many.
The capital city "Sao Paulo" is a city for centuries
is seen embellished with concrete buildings carved pictures of marble
of memoirs of renowned football player 'Pele'
of world-famous stadiums of football.
in the beauteous beaches of city, 'Rio'
nymph-like maidens are seen swimming
"Corcovado" marvellous peak at a distance
Adjacent to it is mountain "Sugar Loss"
Throughout the year people wait
For the carnival of heavenly beauties
In the melodious rhythm of 'Samba'
People cheer up all along the week.

Sau Palo- Rio de Janeiro
2-6 August 2010

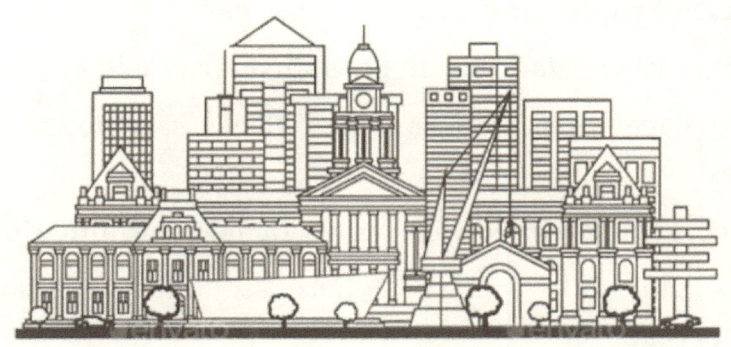

23. Johannesburg

The golden city of black sun

"I am an officer of my street and a power holder of my soul"

So voices the golden city of black sun

What might be the names such as joji, joni, jobarger

Alone peaceful city in the shadow of peaks

Golden mines all around it surrounds

Onto the side is big gutter "ghetto"

In "Soweto" occur cottages of labors like strewn matchboxes

In "Vikalagi" street like diamonds in gravel do occur world peace pigeons

So also residences of noble laureates

Nelson Mandela Desmond Tutu appear

From this very land the fight against apartheid begins

The place where thousands of blacks sacrifice their lives

Once was been filled with murky racial discrimination

Now the white walls of Joberg are filled in black, perpetually

Lakhs of trees occupy the whole city

Its streets take rest in the shadow of "Man-made Forest"

Once the people were united against apartheid

Alas! They are now divided into economic groups

Only, the future could know the repercussions of this change.

Johannes Burg

9 August 2010

24. Cape Town

City of magic

A piece of land that decides geographical beginning and end of the globe

A city which unifies two oceans sweetly

To the West cool breezed Atlantic Ocean

To the East warm Indian Ocean

The landscape of beauties, a rainbow of pomp and gaiety

Red hued sunsets, the lion's roar

Make the visitors appease

And render people a prey to her beauty

For it wears clouds as clothing

The tour on "Table Moutain"

Bestows one the heaven filled happiness

At dusk as darkness pervades over

The moon brims with the beauty

Youthfulness springs among sexy girls
The hidden lust in us hisses over
The magical show "An evening with Cape town"
Is a well-known show known to the world

Cape Town

13 August 2010

25. South Africa

Democratic voice heard

A country that defined

The colours of man

A country that imprisoned

The freedom of the Black race -

A country that is subjected

To the racial discrimination for a long time....

This is where Mahatma Gandhi encountered

Insults and ridicules -

This is where the Black Sun

fought against the racial discrimination.

This is the reality

of the past buried in the present.

It is just now

That the democratic voices are unfolding

In this country of three capitals -

Celebrations of equality are in full swing

And the flowers

of peace are blooming right now.

But hunger still haunts the streets of Soweto

the smoke of the extinguished gunfire
still permeates the surroundings -
With clenched fists and fiery eyes
The blacks who eradicated the apartheid
are ruling the independent nation -
The dragonflies and the butterflies
That took part in the formation of this new nation
Seem lifeless.
It is not an attempt to exhume corpses from cemeteries
It is not an attempt to prick a thorn
in the wound -
But why the past comes to the mind?
What were the hopes of breaking the shackles of slavery? No ideals?
All the dream mansions of the black sun "Madiba" are collapsing
All the voices of pledges and promises seem to be falling apart
Even after the patriarch Mandela left us
To fulfil his aspirations
Let's keep the gates open

Johannes Burg
14 August 2010

26. Simla

Sky and earth throb

The cool hermit is seen inviting with open hands

The seated maiden embellished with divinity

Amorous flower fragrance

Dawns with tender rays of light

It is a place where Earth and sky happen to kiss each other

The beauties of nature are seen blazing in the sunlight

In the cool breeze, breathes the fragrance of sandalwood

The dyke shadowed queue of curved hills

Thick grass greenery embellished with elegant youthfulness

like the amiable touch in the azure sky

the clouds are seen touching the land descending down

the sun is seen inching to embrace the south, slowly

while the night is also seen submerging, slowly

with the lit up lights upon the hillocks

manifest scenes like bubbling stars flown in the sky

a day spent with queen of mountains

embarks in one's infinite experience and a heavenly feeling

Simla
3 July 2009

27. St. Louis

Wearing a Green Sari

America's gateway to the West

On the shores of the scintillating Mississippi River

With the tallest arch in the world

swaying in the air

A wonderful city that welcomes you

With open arms –

Even though it is not a busy cosmopolitan city

It has all the trappings

Of a beautiful city -

A city that hosted a world exhibition a century ago

A city that hosted the Summer Olympics long ago

A city renowned for quality higher education for a long time –

It is the birthplace for King of Beers "Budweiser"

A place of many famous personalities in the history of St. Louis

Harry Truman, T.S Eliot and many more

A city that wears a green sari

It delights one and all

With wonderful restaurants

with floral and sculptural decorations

The city that welcomed us all

Which hosted the World Agriculture Forum

In America's Centre

St. Louis
7 May 2007

28. Niagara

Heavenly bliss

The boisterous flow

fall of water flow from a height, rumbles

and longs to touch the moving clouds

and the flying of white foams, up

a beauteous marvel unable to know thyself

an antic piece which the Nature has carved

from crown of "Mide of Mist"

there appears grand "Skylan Tower", a rainbow bridge

bridges -America - Canada

body- chilling sky flights

admist the moving of dense clouds appear rainbow

which wields the upcoming wind and pierces the clouds

and the fall of heavy dew on one

gives bounty of sport, unlimited happiness

the scenic beauty of Niagara waterfall

fills exuberance in children, happiness in the couples

despite waterfall flow is tremendously

in grandeur, it is seen flowing down

and looks like an angel descending onto the earth from sky

so wondrous

an antic picture unable to be painted

so sweet experience

unforgetful memoir

Niagara waterfall

Is an exaltation where imagination reaches not

Is an exhilaration which any language reaches not

Niagara
12 May 2007

29. New York

Sleepless City

On one side, glittering beauties kiss the sky

On the other, in the dark tunnels the lights of highway

To the side Corporate buildings of market, "Empire State Building,"

"Rockfeller" centre

murky streets full of mafia group such as "Harlem" "Brakes"

Onto the other

On one side grand goods' display centres

Gardens on the edges onto the other

The eye glittering "Broadway"

What is said to be Avenue of America

A city endows with diversity of life

For centuries five, the city holds its stardom

In the tall buildings, lit with neon lights

The city knows not what is said to be a respite

One learns not its greatness

Unless it is visited once

In this city where sleep is unknown

With clubs and theatres entertainment is all

Every a second is a paradise of pomp and gaiety

At Madison or Time squares any acquaintance happens to come across

None can speak due to the din of people

Ground zero commemorates

three thousand martyrs who got victimized in the hands of terrorists

the Statue of Liberty in Ellis island

expo American - France friendship

onto the side of it is "Hudson" river

is seen piercing into fog like a sleek hill

for the mass who come from New Jersy through subways,

the sun greets them with warm welcome, at dawn

and at the dusk, in their return journey

the lights of neon stars bid them adieu

can't it be inevitable to bid adieu

for a city that knows not sleep!

New York

14 May 2007

30. Varanasi

The city God built for himself

Kasi, Varanasi, Benaras... whatever name is attributed to it
is an old city with no dawn of birth and dusk of death
a city older than history, Puranas
a hermitage God built for himself
the strive of Bhagirath makes it possible on this land
obtains sanctity on banks of the pious Ganga river
the holy place where Sathya Harischandra himself been sold out
for the sake of truth and dharma
a pilgrimage known for Hindu way of life
bath ghats, temples, festivals at Varanasi
have been the symbols of culture and tradition
of chant of Vedas at early morning in Kasi
of the broadcast of "His Master Voice" from heaven
aids it as an epicentre of all disciplines, knowledge and spirituality
birth place of bards like Tulsidas, Kabir, Ravidas
an abode for Buddhists, Jains and Mohmads

a cherished pilgrimage for every Hindu in one's life time

a perihelion travelogue for earthly paradise

                                          Varanasi

                                    14 April 1999

31. Kolkata

The synergy of equality and love

The very land of Goddess Kali

A jewel in the British Crown once

A garland of equality grown out of struggles as on the day

For reason knows not thy be darling of all

Of which tales the authors have penned,

of which poems are ebbed

of which nobler modes of lives

of which scholarly maidens

have longed to live in you

thy embrace all such in thy bosom with open hands

thou hide them not only in thy heart but also in thy soul

The very jewel of Goddess Kali

a unique union of the East and the West

a mixture of modern cultures

a heavenly abode of book lovers and senior citizens

with the music concert of Ravindra on the hanging bridge

the amorous voice of the intellectuals manifests

though you were declared as city of silence

have been seen running to the past glory

and have been facing contemporary issues

The roads are filled with dust

in the summer the blazing sunlights

peoples' life stream is seen halted due to sporadic rains

The population is seen swelling day by day

every day there are open public meetings

where noisy claims of political leaders to achieve humanity

despite it is the abode of intellectuals

goddess Kali is studded with glittering nose ring

the land has been soaked with love of Mother Theresa

the intermix of equality and affections' gist is city Calcutta

That's the reason why you are a darling of all

for the one of today and the day before ones'

Kolkata

15 May 1996

32. Karachi

City under military shadows

It is a city of star-studded lights

A mega city seen swelling without a plan

The huge old buildings built during the British rule

Despite visiting for the first time

All the countenances are acquainted with

On the very visages of them

Seen Iqbal who quoted "of all the better of world, Hindustan is the best"

Is uttered on their mouths

Has felt as if I met Faiz Ahmed Faiz

Whom I met in Beriut some years ago

Even the much-cherished democratic military chief

Zulfikar Ali Bhutto was appeared to be there in the crowd

And searched for Tharik Ali

Whom I happened to meet as "Trotskyite"

in New Delhi a decade ago

Those people, those streets

Are not appearing new to me
And felt living in Mumbai and Hyderabad
Despite
Pakistan has ushered a new dawn
In the Father of Nation Jinnah's city
No such exuberance is seen
In the morning,
from the news read of "The Dawn" one will be of opinion
violence has been seen as an activity of every day there
to such an opinion one will easily get to
people are scared of what would happen every time
and that destruction may be greater than the previous one
an agony shall not these destructions be obliterated
in fact with gripping fear I roamed in the city
have visited Quaid-e-Azam tombs
On meeting an American University friend
the world renowned Islamic Scholar
Syed Hussain Jafri,
there came aspect of 'Muhajirs' life
Of the secrets unknown to anyone
The truths never seen hidden despite striving to hide
the city is seen with millions of hopes

just, has been yielding to the dying ideals
so as to evoke the hope of living in ones
having been burning the seconds one awaits
the 'Muhazirs' are seen collecting the fragmented souls
one would feel pity for the very sigh of the city Karachi
but this is an undeniable truth
Nation is under the shadow of military control
You, Pakistan! Pardon me for my understanding you like this
Never think what matters to a visitor
since I long for universal fraternity
Am I not your neighbour?
With many a hardship I have come here
may not be visiting again.
No hope that I would come again
Throw away the network of terrorism
and broadcast the aroma of humanity
in the parched lands of your desert
The lilies of affection are viewed not
and shower the rain of democracy
take hold of my olive hand
Be it a defeat or be it a victory it pertains to both
obliteration of terrorism would be good for both of us

Usher the fallen consciousness

Shake the tired democracy

Only that is your weapon; use it once again

Such is my salutation to you

Karachi

24 January 1985

33. Vienna

World music capital

Long ago five centuries before the birth of Lord Christ

It is a city that established along the banks of River Danube

It is the seat of Afro- Hungarian kingdom

It is the youthful city /though was established in ancient times

It reflects the spirit of the age amidst the visitors

Where the streets are filled with noise of horse neighing

It is the heartthrob of European literature and culture

Where the world renowned singers have been singing to melodious chords

It is a birth place of "Mozart", "Strauss", "Beethoven"

For over centuries it has been the capital of musical world

So it is said in the streets of Vienna dance gnome is seen walking wobbly

To watch the bygone glory of the city

the streets are embellished with marvellous buildings

the glee gale gentle breezes at the edges of mountains

the murmur of flower petals , showers, and melodious music

extend warm welcome to the visitors

then at the point has stricken in me somewhere read word

the most beautiful city of the world is Vienna!

Vienna
22 June 1984

34. Danube River

Beauty of royalty

The very queen European rivers

Having been born in the Black-Forest of the West

Till the submersion of it into the black sea in the East

Does travel three thousand kilometers among nations ten

In each of the nation with ever new fashions it travels

The bubbling brook in each nation gives new sort of sound

With running flow of water it is known as River of newness, ever

On the either side of the river flow, occupy the thick forests

Blue hued foam, runs and crazes are seen all-round

Its flow is seen in dimensions of huge, slow, and elegantly

It is the relative testimony to the European history

and is also the nervous system of transactions'

with giggling sounds of the incessant water flow

infuses spirit in poets and singers

onto the West a threshold for Mangolian and Turkish invansion

the unchanging steady flow despite of occurrence of battles and agony

it witnesses' of the establishments of several royal dynasties and their obliteration

its flow is seen exhibiting amorous

like a maiden of underground water world

in azure hue the water volunteers its flow

Danube river
24 June 1984

35. Munich

A good combination of old and new

The twelfth century city established on banks of river Isar

The threshold for baleriya alf Mountain range

The peace abode of " Benedictine" sages

The world renowned city which knows not the rest

A city which even enables to even hear a dropping drop

In Munich even the language sings

It accomplishes chords to the songs which linger in air

Surprisingly from concrete also grows the grass

A mixture of old and new customs and marvellous buildings

An authority in the domains of literature and tradition

Beauty bustles in the so-called "October Fest"

Where youth consume millions of litres of beer

When one walks in the streets memoir of ghostly acts of terrorists reflect

1972 Winter Olympics debacle is displayed

The guide happens to comment it has reflected the blazing sunshine

Of the history of the centuries old Olympic games

Munich remains as a bitter memory

Munich
14 June 1984

36. Cologne

The structure of human ingenuity

On either side of River Rhine

The historical city of Sages been established in the first century

There where cradles civilization of man

The beauty of Cologne and picnics in river Rhine

Is profound

Even the emperors who believed themselves to be gods

Participate in the excursions on the River Rhine

With marvellous speed, agility and subtleness

Flows river Rhine

Surpassing the hillocks, forests, plains

And all along boring the secrets of forts

The murky streets that are filled with foul smell and dust

Repair drowning them with floods

A German poet opines that it is safeguarding the prestige of Coloan

In the world wars too, it did not get deterred

"The Catholic Cathedral" is the primer crown of the city

Would invite the visitors standing straight
and peeping up right into it
It was built with tender hands and loveable heart
An epitome of human skill

Cologne
28 June 1984

37. The Berlin Wall

Dumb Witness

There stands a dividing wall bisecting Berlin's heart into two

That unsympathetic one stands among the amiable brothers

On either side of it they happen to remain

With burning heart they watch the boulder wall

Their hearts aren't stones

Their blood isn't colourless water

So why are they sighing?

Sighing and heartthrob and upon heartthrob are sighing

Though their souls long for breaking it

It is one of the materials made without life

It is crude poison which knows not how to console them

Whose mistake might it be it is being erected by men, only

Somebody inflicted the fire and some other aggravated it

Betrayals, traitors and hatemongers erected it

That erected wall symbolizes their revenge

It is historical one that witnesses man's murkiness silently

A helpless, lifeless wall built with boulders

Is said to be the wall of Berlin

West Berlin

29 June 1984

38. Geneva

Naturally beautiful city

The tiny mega city of the world

An address for natural elegance

A city where millions of visitors take respite

A permanent residence for thousands of foreigners

Exquisite display of Alps Mountains

A threshold that welcomes with olive branches

A residence for several International Organizations

This is place where the seed for brotherhood

among the countries of world is laid

this is a place where universal man and humanity seeds were sowed

this is the place where

roots have been laid for mutual cooperation among the countries of the world

it is a natural city

it is a city where refugees are consoled who suffered due to tyranny

it is a city which beckons lights in the lives of destitutes

with witnesses of dew and with green hued beauties

it is a city which broadcasts fragrance of humanity

it is a fragrance of flower bloomed for achieving the world peace

it is a heaven on this very land featuring fragrance, melody and peace

Geneva

1 July 1984

39. Switzerland

A place of knowledge

A marvellous beauteous nation it is
Where its people long for peace, over there
Alps Mountains are seen hovering with fluffy clouds
Where cool breezes and warm showers
Are seen melting the silver coated mountains
And upon mountain peaks been embellished with grass plains
Its green grasslands spread like turf
And the rivers are seen running amidst the mountains
Despite the mountains are lifeless
They do stand as a wall against greedy and hatred of humans

It is a place of prudence
Where love, peace and brotherhood prevail
Amidst vast herbage
Where love and joy happen to reach their zenith
Over here, universal self- confidence resides
The heaven on this very land

Jungfraujoch
2 July 1984

40. Copenhagen

Address for honesty

With glittering complexion of forgetful opium

The elegant ladies with their lose hair are seen roaming in the streets

In the winter over here

The sun dares not to come out

Despite the roads being filled with snow

during the days as well as nights there is bustle of people

when one watches the golden hue of sun

during the dawn of summer

however one awaits the sun reaches not to hug the horizon of west

even at night ten '0' clock also sun is in the streets

and has been seen watching to the

Hilarious shouts of the youth and elegant ladies

who ride bicycles crazily

Solidarity is the culture of the people over here

over here equality is the least bothered aspect

the aspect of punctuality people like and honesty is the policy of people

over here health security is free to all its people

but unfortunately, the government taxes are quite high

Copenhagen
3 July 1984

41. Amsterdam

Jewellery for beauty

In the thirteenth century it was born

River Amstel is its birth place

Wherever sighted it is beautiful

Happiness on all the possible directions

People of Amsterdam need no cars or bikes

For them bicycle is very dear

The hut boat residences are seen floating on the waters

The street musical concerts are seen merging in air

Patience is the virtue of its inhabitants

The ever-peeping droplets of sea breezes
Freshly, comfortably and happily people of this city do
I

                                        Amsterdam
                                        5 July 1984

42. Belgium

Throne of Ideals

O honourable human Victorian!

I offer my salutations to your tired feet

That got injured in the world wars

And greetings to your merit and talent

The battle of super power nations in the pursuit for supremacy

Despite ruined, you to state of excavations mercilessly

Though they have been the cause to shed your innocent blood

Despite your happiness is destroyed

Thy flag of victory still flutters in the sky

O Belgium!

You happen to be the care of address

For self-confidence and pure devotion

A home for destitute

A throne for ideals

Having faced the fate and with its marvellous patience

It is a nation which is growing beyond one's expectations

Its capital Brussels is a historical city

But it is city upgraded with modernity

It is a dream city for artists and poets

A hub for gaiety and entertainment

A place for multiple cultures

Its each building symbolizes beauty

It gives excitement to visitors

Brussels
6 July 1984

43. Paris

The city of cosmic love

The only city in the world that sleeps not any day ever

A city known for amorous sex

It is not only city meant for poets and artists

It is also a love city for lovers too

During the day a perfume bottle, and at night a bottle of champagne

It is a home for the fashion world

For delicate neck of Paris River pine is a stone studded necklace

Its crown is Eifel tower

For shying first dusk it is seen providing the lights

Like a queen stands there with dignity

The visitors who have come from all around world

Are seen roaming in the streets of Paris

When taking respite in the shadow of "Iron Lady"

Adjacent to it the world famous "Notrodo" "Luvra' Museums

Happen to look at them with jealousy

Despite being tired though

Some of the visitors are seen framing their experiences climbing up

When one sights deeply her wobble looking body in the evening dusk

The birds like the daughters of sky are seen flying over her.

And happen to show the path to heaven

During the sunset the golden rays fall on her

The fountain of these glistening lights

Showers lights upon the city

In these sizzling lights when one is about to sleep

The noise at night annoys the Eifel tower

When one peeps into "Louvre" Museum adjacent to it

It lures one with its glaring looks

While watching the painting of merciful Mona Lisa

" Place de la Concorde " the world famous opera, " Palais Garnier "

"Garden canal", " Place du Palais Royal " of many such

When one is seen singing an evening in the Paris

While walking in the streets of " Avenue des Champs-Élysées"

One will attain such happiness as if he conquered the world

On the banks of the river pine displays blissful beauties

At the midnight in aris

Wonderful dream stunts shows like "Moulin Rouze", "Lido"

Wondrous display of sophisticated technology

The never forgetful experience in one's life time

Paris
9 July 1984

44. Versailles Palace

Venus favoured palace

The stony constructions of middle ages

Are wonderful, marvellous and surprising

They demonstrate the dignity of monarchy

The active welcoming statue of the horse which is seen glaring at sky

And the beautiful decorated antics ambience

The colourful films

The statues of "versless" bring reputation to it

With features of awesome, ecstasy and enchanting

This wealth of artefacts bears sensitive touch of life

Some of these are offered to God

Always, Venus happens to be the premier goddess

The crystal clear palace over here reflects the glory of the past

Both war and peace jointly achieved palace it is

Versailles

10 July 1984

45. London

The city of rich people

The city that knows not respite, is city Victoria

A crowned city of emperors and kings

Sinks with dense population, ever busy is the central London

Vast green landscapes adjacent to it

Huge glass wheeled "London Eye"

Gigantic clock tower tilting "Big Ben Bay"

Solitude and strong statue of Napoleon the Great

The building which reined the British Empire upon whose one the Sun never sets "West minister"

The residence of Prime Ministers for generations is "10 Downing"

For centuries, known as Royal Crown, "Buckingham Palace"

A city known to speak languages of more than three hundred

A city known for affections

A city which inhabits with royal rich families

A city which holds musical concerts all through the seasons

A city that everyone longs to visit

A city ever green in memory in one's life.

London
14 September 1978

46. Thames

Royal river

The grandeur of royalty is the Thames
Being born at Gloster Hyer
It flows in length and breadth across the city of London
And is seen stiflingly merging in the North Sea
it travels for over four ten scores of mile
its waves clamor around seven metres
of merger of around twenty sub-rivulets it is perpetual
oxford, reading, hinli, have been established on it
eye-appeasing windstar, kingstral, richmon appear on its banks
gorgeous scenes of landscapes on either side of it

the scene of paired sawn swimming
the beauteous rowing boats scene
still more beautiful scene, is of, cheer girl dance
for centuries along as royal crown
Thames stands tall all in all.
death in kasi takes one on to the path of liberation

Thames River, London
14 September 1978

47. Rome

Not built in a day

Rome is an Empire known for royalty

The darling of my dreams for over years, is this city

Gorgeous buildings' caricatures appear on the elevated land

The eye catching Italy's scenic beauties

The wondrous display of waves across the ocean

Just been experiencing the gentle breeze

That was what Caesar experienced once

As a witness of yester years

There lay, wretched towers, dilapidated buildings

In the permeating sunrays

The glory of Empire of Italy is seen over here just

Of the thirst of emperor's expansion of empire

The dust merges with aesthetic pleasure over here

Will display the bygone glory of this city

On the seats of these royal buildings

The carved floor is seen with varied colours

Up upon the roofs of the tall buildings, are seen carverd monuments

It Is an ineffable experience

In the moonlit light

Thy beauty is never seen before and indescribable

O the city of Rome!

It is true you weren't built in a day

While walking in the streets of bygone kingdom

The fragrance of thy yesteryears glory

Made my soul dance fondly

Rome
20 July 1984

48. Florence

Capital of the arts

The grand griddle of Italy is Florence

Is the very place of resurrection

The birth place of several poets and great many more sculptures,

Many a painter and many more philosophers

Is a city where " Dante Alighieri", "Michelangelo",

"Leonardo Da Vinci", "Sandro Botticelli", "Raphael"

Opened their eyes

It is the place

Where people like Picasso and several others obtained cubism

The great old commercial complexes of Florentine

And gorgeous monuments have been built over here

Is the place where David received apprenticeship in hands of "Michelangelo"

O the worlds' hereditary treasure! You appear on the bank of river Arno

Thou have been distributing beauteous

cozy nest palaces all around

With Pitti Palace on the shore of Arno

Thy one, owns the glory of Monalisa

So only why thou are the capital city of arts!

Florence

23 July 1984

49. Kashmir

Heaven on earth

Thy presence is known for Himalayas
And is known as treasure of natural scenic beauty
The empire of royal patronage
A kaleidoscopic villa of heaven on earth
The sky kissing Mahogany trees
The wind that gushes from elevated pine trees
dreams infusing and eye-touching view of tulip garden
Rainbow hued flower fragrance
The chirping of several kinds of birds
Amidst the snow-capped hills
The brook's sounds of bent waterfalls
Embellishwd with beauteous valleys, lush green grass lands
The dike oriented path travelogue

While there is snow shower
It will acquire new beauties
And does offer a warm welcome to the visitors

Srinagar
23 June 1983

50. Bangkok

Place for amorous lovers

People, people wherever you see
Vast number of people covering the very edges of city
It is densely populated, there is dearth of room
So only why the city is becoming a dungeon of pollution
Never ending chaos, depletion of oxygen
Yet, the city is expanding with every tickle of clock
The city on the whole is in doldrums
The visitors throng in the city

It is a lovely place to visit once
But unpleasant one for inhabiting
Huge sex rocketing
Of against the established law
And for crazy lovers
The whole city is filled with liquor shops and massage centers
The business of prostitution is seen patronized
Every day it witness murders, burglary, hores treading
Often the common people are victimized.

Bangkok
3 October 1982

51. Philippines

Pleasure of nature

Thy Island beckons

With premier touch of eastern earth rays

The country is credited with the premier dawn of the globe

A country seen welcoming the tourists

With great attractions, exuberance

Mesmerizes the people

Is an island of heaven

Possessing age old woods

Wide ranged trees

The glittering waters of rivers

The warmth of Mother Nature

All are special attraction for visitors

An American military base in Asia

The dictatorial policies of the rulers

The people who cherish their goal with aid of Americans

Of the family rule of "Atheno"

Bribery is seen lurking everywhere

Maybe all these linger in the ears of visitors

So only why this is a special country

Where visitors strive to be happy and get experienced?

On the banks of "Malena" the sunset is a special attraction

The tali azure on the top

Of distancing boats on grounded banks

At a distance green hillocks

Will gush with golden hue

Where the sun is seen flying away

The dawn's beauties

The unforgettable Manila memories

Manila

7 October 1982

52. Mecca

Wash away sins!

This pious city is endowed with wide streets
Tall houses built with whitewash constitute it.
And around every corner appear as narrow lanes
Houses are scanty
Hills, hillocks, valleys encircle the city
Beside the buildings built over hundred years ago
Modern sky scrapers catch one's sight
In this uninhabited block rock valley

A ray of hope is ushered

Of the aspect of cleansing sins of man

Obsessed with such faith

Since time immemorial till today

Every street of this city

Echoes with the prayer, "Allah Hu Akbar"

Every street welcomes the pilgrims

Pilgrims from all continents visit this pious place

During the nights of hustle - bustle free streets

The harking mouths are seen relished with tea

Here pilgrims sit for long hours

And experience the memories of yesteryears

They never appear disappointed about the contemporary issues

And hold its past glory ever, such is the city Mecca

Mecca

3 July 1981

53. Sandstorms

Even mocking the mountains

I am a sand dune that knows not concern, mercy

I am faithless, untrained natural calamity

Desert is my mother, wind is my father

I hide in any a harrow

I appear at all right occasions

Slowly, gently, I speed up myself

And sleep on the bosom of sun who present the day to dear earth

in yellow hue I grow tall

Like a tiger I roar

Capable of attacking mightier than it

I leave my indelible impact on the

And would erase the old alphabet carved on it

I perform ceremony

For unidentified skeletons

And would convert small heaps of gravel into mounds

I take pleasure

In challenging mountains that take pride in guard

I count not the hurdles

Such as thorns, bushes, hills in my odyssey

Of the fragrance of my very arrival

The people walking along roadways

Would run to reach their destinations

Pomp and gaiety also run away

The thunder, like a gentle music chord

Would announce the very arrival of me

With bustle of huge sound like a large ballad

I do dance like Lord Shiva

I would cause the devastation

And will enjoy the sight of man's doom.

Dammam

2 June 1980

54. Saudi Arabia

Home of Peace

In this country

No political gimmicks

No sight of political hawks

It uses not people's exchequer

In this country

No drinks that cause hangover

No drugs, no rapes

In this country

No black market

No adulteration of food items

No hike of prices that try to touch the sky
In this country
No destructive terrorists
No signs of violence or agitations
No traces of innocent people's deaths
In this country
No half-naked dances, no pub feats
No room for gambles
Not an iota of prostitution
In this country
No underground mafia
No mining mafia
No religious disputes
In this country
No factionalism
No rowdyism
No gundaism at all
In this country
No burglaries
No middlemen, no cheats
No red carpet treatment for law breakers
In this country
No gang rapes
No bribery
No bank loan evaders

In this country
No strikes
No bandhs
No gheraos as such
In this country
No breaking of traffic rules
No encroachment of lands
No mercy plea of any criminal
In this country
No land scams
No gobbling by sages
No bomb scares
In the language of the world, this country
Is known as an apostle of democracy
Where dictatorial governance
Hierarchy and Aristocracy whatsoever
Things that lead man to crime and violence
Are not found here
In this country no such people are seen
What if there is no democracy here?
So claim the common people of Saudi

Riyadh
3 May 1980

55. Africa

The diversity of life

A continent that was

Created by God with an explosion aeons ago,

In the dark forests

Where even the light rays cannot enter

Hidden, are the great mysteries of humanity.

The sun's rays pierce the darkness of the forest

Strong waves hit the shores of the oceans

Sand swells between the toes on the shores

Hills full of green vines

Touch the blue sky.

Trees are covered in delicate mauve cloth
Shrubs are dressed in brown
The voice of God can be heard in the thunder
The scent of rain clouds is the breath
Of the raindrops.
The continent of dinosaurs
that saw the evolution of the ages
is famous for biodiversity
for biological habitat.
Life itself was originated here
This is where the human race orirginated.
A free space for enthusiasts and guides
This place with the sound
of the breeze in the woods continues
to purify the body.
A temple of geniuses and miracles
A place of peace and serenity
It is a unique continent that gives life to millions of hopes

Khartoum

12 October 1978

56. Sudan

Of course, an ordinary country, except

The borrowed culture of Arabs

It appears like a roughly stitched quilt.

Uncertainty, laziness prevail in this country

Despite being endowed with infinite Natural resources

Alas, it depends on debts every day

A country which runs for fresh debts without clearing old ones, ever

In spite of being born on the same Earth, fails to live unitedly

In the South inhabit black Catholic Christians

And in the North, inhabit Arabs who adore Allah

The villages all along the banks of river Nile

And their people are seen quarrelling
And seen flowing along the current,
But from its capital "Khartoum"
Pathetic village tales must be listened to.
The River Nile flows with no hustle and bustle.

Khartoum
12 October 1978

57. Yasser Arafat

Head of state without country

Yasser Arafat, a glowing star

Blooms in the Land of God

It is an abode of several religions and faiths

A voice of Palestine

Constitutes many a land of workmanship

Just to give birth to his mother land.

For some, he is a terrorist

For others, he is a man who cannot be understood

A leader for a nation that exists not

He ekes out life with a tight rope around his neck,

Overcomes the danger of murder every a day

Having started war with 'Arafat'

Offers olive branch to settle with United Nations Organization

For having professed non-violence pleas.

Arafat, receive our salutations.

After demise of Yasser Arafat on 11 November 2002

In remembrance of meeting him in Beirut on 3 May 1976 along with

Captain Prem Singh, First Secretary, Indian Embassy in Beirut

58. George Habash

Beloved leader of Palestine

George Habash

Is known as Palestinians' liberation zeal

He resides in the heart of Israel as a nightmare

Mere protests and revolts

Actually, acknowledges not the truth, keeps not the justice

Amidst birth and mortality and relics of excavations

Is seen to have roamed among bloodshed places

And credited to have scripted the paths of revolt

Abandoning the teachings, precepts

And getting sharp weapons

In the battle of weapons, he believes that

There won't be any scope for white flag

Having been boycotting peace talks

Thy are the soldiers who waged

An uncompromised war against the enemy

Known as knight he shoulders the gun as his virtue

Of whom Arabs are seen calling him dearly as "Al Hakim"

After demise of George Habash on 26 January 2008
In remembrance of seeing him on 0 March 1976 at a rally in Beirut

59. Petra

Pink city

Aloofness, happiness and tenderness

All such features are intermixed in this beautiful historical city

In the remote desert

A man carved the red mountain and built this pink city

The very kingdom reigned by the "Nabatains" with their magical wand

A renowned commercial center two thousand years ago

A natural calamity has stricken it

And succumbed to the devastating earthquake

People are scattered

But this pink city bowed not

Even in the state of lifeless

The soft tender "Korenthiak" shrines of it are damaged not

Despite the blazing sun been wounded thy rocks

Old temples, palaces of Kingdoms, treasury buildings

Even today are seen glittering

The moon takes delight in showering moonlight on the statues and sculptures

Petra

5 August 1977

60. Cyprus

Beautiful island

In the Mediterranean's

Gorgeous ambience is the island of Cyprus

An abode of Greek love Goddess "Afradites" birth place it is

Amidst Roman Mosaics', Phoenician tombs

Lie tall mountains in the veil of tall pine tress

Valleys adorned with green bushes

Are seen with wonderful beaches

The azure sky without clouds

At a juncture when Sun is seen kissing the sky

Amidst the chirping of the birds

A gorgeous displayed to watch

While travelling one would glimpse the beauty of heavenly queen

All of a sudden our journey got a break

There appeared a "Green Line"

It bisects the country; it is called to a Green Line

Untouched by the "Line" emanates the aroma of white lilies

Showers much fragrance on either side of the line

But on either side of the line,

the land is seen crushed under heavy boots of Greek and Turkey soldiers

on either directions sounds of bullets

hatred, revenge

not just land is divided

there is a division among people as well

In the North Mosques and in the South, Churches

in no aspect coordination is seen between them

The so-called man needs to love one's own country

That's what our elders said.

but their native place is divided into two;

Which piece of land should I love?

This is the question my Cyprus friend is haunted by.

Despite this fact, he is an optimist

The grasslands bloom with promise

In near future on white horse one will be seen whiling with

From "Sydash" to forlorn in grass lands

It is said love goddess has been visiting her birthplace

In this Island that got separated into North and South poles

When does this cyclone end?

In this gorgeous island when can one breathe freedom?

O friend!

I will look forward to such a sweet moment

I will visit again to listen to the chords of grasslands

Nicosia

2 October 1976

61. Palmyra

Address to Royalty

Palmyra is a city that died long ago

Today it is lifeless artefact

Though its rose hue is wondrous beauty

A testimony to the bygone kingdoms that cherished beauty

Then rolled out royal diamonds

Blood dropped to the ground due to tyranny

As on today there are no kings and no commands

But in this universe thy glory lies in the excavations

Amidst this desert thou on lone glitter

And hold the visitors spellbound
When the sun is seen showering light on
her sleeping visage her smile fades not
Like a star that has lost no light its glory is still beaming
Despite her stunning beauty being robbed by violent storms
her royal dignity was never at low ebb
the ray taken birth out of big bang
is seen glistening through her excavations
it was once reigned by Meditararian, Persian kings
Today you remain in silence and dignity
Now, only the perpetually praying mosque remains
The kingdom was established by Roman and "Queen Zenobia "
what is thy position in it?
Why are the marble statues not seen? Where are those golden toys?
Where are queen Zenobia's crowns?

Palmyra
5 August 1977

62. Faiz Ahmed Faiz

Addiction

The progressive creative literary leader of undivided India

The heart-broken lover whose poetry journeyed onto the people's poetry

With the inspiration of progressive writers movement like Anjamun Tarraqi Pasand Mussanifin-e-hind

Aims to build a new world with aiming goals and aspirations

Beholding the torch of communism, he surpasses all the directions

This poetic flower happened to set his foot in the tumultuous Pakistan

Having been crushed under tyranny

With wounded wounds and in the lap of defeat
With enormous chords and holding his fist upright
Poetic resentment as a weapon
A destined man who voices the destiny of democracy
A poet of people who aspires people's welfare
He thought of creating a whirlpool for sake of people
Thought of sharpening the sword of protest
Spreading the awareness of Palestine struggle
The world nomadic who is seen fighting all alone
In the prohibited streets
At times when explosions and gloom are seen spreading
At times when colossal destructions are taking place
On the bank of meditararian sea
At a time when religion is seen devastating the humanity
Despite our religions are different
The blazing flow of poesy
Is seen with Faiz the ambassador of Humanity
Their acquaintance and handshake is a sort of art
Faiz poem is a sort of memorization
And is a wave of experience of Mediterranean Sea

Riyadh
22 March 1985

In remembrance of meeting Faiz long ago in Beirut and knowing his demise of 20 November 1984

63. Beirut

Paris of the east

Thou is the fine pearl of Meditararian Sea

A hub of all earthly entertainment

Thou the most beauteous city of the land

A form of international women

It is a hub for freedom and happiness

Where dissipation knows not respite

Thou the night Jasmine of the world of Lord Indra

Boundless delights and happiness

Delightful dinners and entertainments

When one wakes up

In reality do you ever happen to sleep to wake up

This is the Paris of the East

But is the best when compared to London, Paris and New York

With the onset of dusk, manna movements start

It ushers one's youthfulness

The eye-blinding lights

Distinguishes no difference between day and night

What has happened there?

On a day while one is drowsy due to the musical concerts

Upon thy white hued life

Having been fired the pistols

Who is the one, has penned the blood inked lines on it

The people happened to remain like onlookers in their very sleep

In a city where even foreigners are supposed to move freely

Under the patrol of pistols the people are seen roaming with their bowed heads

It is enough to victimize the lives for thy beauty

Now, do wake up from the ruined rocks?

It is not of bombs, bullets and kidnappings

Humanity and affection need to bloom again and again

Beirut

20 December 1975

64. Lebanon

The pleasure place of the Arabs

A country embellished with mysteries of mankind

A centre for alphabet

Blissfully, capital of it, sustains for over thousands of years

Where civilization of Phoenicians flourishes

Having acquired the doctrine of the skill of navigation

A gorgeous country, as Switzerland of Mediterranean Sea it is called so

A cosy as well as lovely one amidst revered countries of the World

Onto the left of it is sea, on to the right is a mountain range

And behind green covered mountains snow hillocks appease

And "Skating" the mountains within half an hour

One would enjoy "swimming" on the shore of Mediterranean.

A calm country, appeases the visitors fully

The tall Cedar trees charm all

And onto the beaches river of it does flow lavishly

Snow-capped mountains are found nearby

A country to be relished along with family

A country where Arabs visit for luxuries and merriment

Amidst the kingdoms of Arabs, the lone country of Christians

It's an iconic country for all Arabs.

Beirut
16 December 1975

www.ingramcontent.com/pod-product-compliance
Lightning Source LLC
LaVergne TN
LVHW041946070526
838199LV00051BA/2920